THANK YOU
COACH

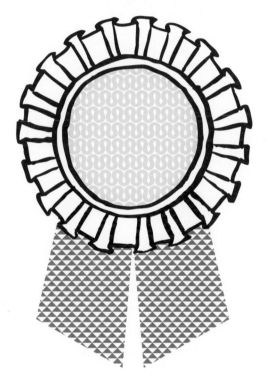

PaRragon

Bath • New York • Cologne • Melbourne • Delhi
Hong Kong • Shenzhen • Singapore • Amsterdam

This book is a

BIG

THANK YOU

to you,

for encouraging me
so much this year ...

And because you've supported me
A LOT this year, I've drawn a
picture of you:

I WANT TO
THANK YOU
FOR YOUR ...

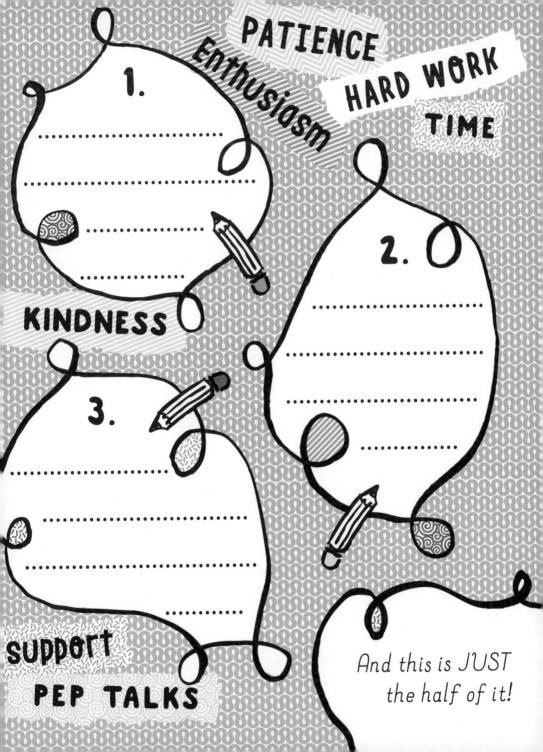

1.
....
....
....
....

PATIENCE

Enthusiasm

HARD WORK

TIME

2.
....
....
....
....

KINDNESS

3.
....
....
....

SUPPORT

PEP TALKS

And this is JUST the half of it!

1.

They help you
hone your skills.

2. They **motivate** you
(and stop you from giving up).

3. They help you set CLEAR GOALS.

One of mine is to: ....

....

....

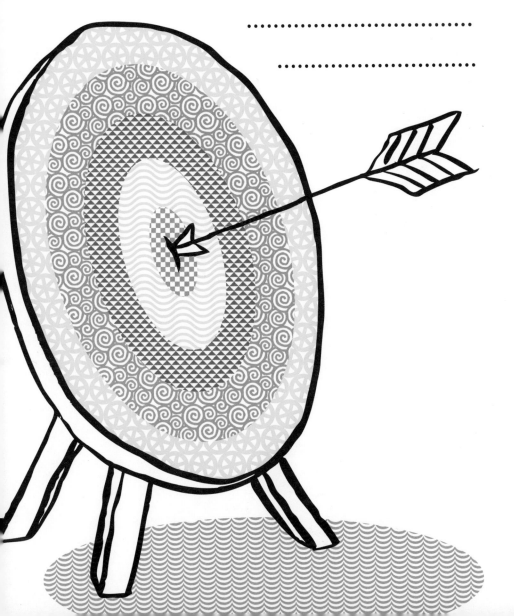

4. They help you work on things you want to **do better**.

5. And they help you to improve your STRENGTHS!

They all involve

WORKING

TOGETHER!

... IN FACT,
I think you're
pretty **AWESOME!**

BEFORE you were
my coach, I had
A LOT TO LEARN.

But this is me AFTER I met you.

Now!

Really Confident
& REALLY good at:...

....

Since training **with you,** I have become **MORE:**

and **less:**

1st

So, you see, you're an _inspiration!_

My new motto is:

THE COACH IS ALWAYS RIGHT.

Even when I said "I can't," you knew **I COULD.**

Here's a cheer about the greatest coach:

....

....

....

....

....

....

....

....

....

You have shown me what I'm **naturally good at**, as well as some things **I didn't think I could do!**

My **THREE**
GREATEST VICTORIES
with you have been ...

1. ....
....
....
2. ....
....
....
3. ....
....
....

As the saying goes,

Actions speak LOUDER than words.

But some of your words are REALLY LOUD, too.

Here are some of the WORDS that you OFTEN use with me:

The award for
BEST COACH
goes to:

· ·

for:

· ·

· ·

· ·

· ·

THANK YOU ⭐

GRACIAS

DANKE

DZIĘKUJĘ

Grazie

TACK

Merci

KIITOS

Grazzi

OBRIGADO

→ HVALA

From:

. . . .

signature

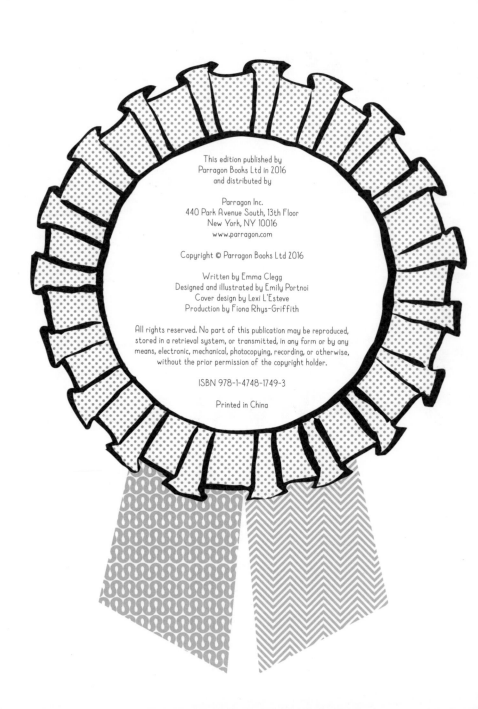

This edition published by
Parragon Books Ltd in 2016
and distributed by

Parragon Inc.
440 Park Avenue South, 13th Floor
New York, NY 10016
www.parragon.com

Written by Emma Clegg
Designed and illustrated by Emily Portnoi
Cover design by Lexi L'Esteve
Production by Fiona Rhys-Griffith

ISBN 978-1-4748-1749-3

Printed in China